Understanding
Inflation
Accounting

by Timothy S. Lucas
FASB Project Manager

Financial Accounting Standards Board

Library of Congress Cataloging in Publication Data
Lucas, Timothy S.
   Understanding Inflation Accounting

   Bibliography: p. 81
   1. Inflation Accounting. I. Title.
81-66859

ISBN 0-07-020830-1

Purpose

Recently published annual reports for large public U.S. companies include some unfamiliar information—information about the effects of inflation and changing prices. This information is being produced as a result of a new accounting standard that recognizes the power of price changes to blunt the usefulness of traditional accounting reports. However, the new information produced as a result of the standard can be useful only if it is understood.

This book is a springboard to understanding information about the effects of inflation and specific price changes. It explains how companies are reporting the information and how it might be used and interpreted. The book has been written for people who read the annual reports of large companies, particularly people who are not experts in the technical aspects of accounting. These people have various reasons for their interest in annual reports. Some are interested in buying or selling stock. Some are lenders who are concerned with credit worthiness. Some hold positions in government and need information about the prosperity of business as a basis for setting economic policies. Some are interested because they are employees or advisors of others who have more direct interests. For all these people, the new information opens the door to a better understanding of business at a time when prices are changing. We hope this book will help in realizing the potential of that information.

This book is an attempt to explain some complex concepts in simple and nontechnical terms. To do that, it introduces a number of simple situations in which a business has only a few assets and transactions. While the situations are admittedly unrealistic, they illustrate the meaning of concepts such as income. Those concepts are no different when applied to real financial reports that aggregate thousands or even millions of individual transactions.

Acknowledgements

This book has been prepared with the counsel of the following members of the FASB's Users Task Group:

Vincent S. Castellano - Goldman, Sachs & Co.
Anthony T. Cope - Wellington Management Company
William S. Easman, Jr. - Easman Inflation
   Consultants, Inc.
Edward W. Gabrielski - First National Bank of Boston
David Hale - Kemper Financial Services, Inc.
David F. Hawkins - Harvard Business School
Robert Levine - Kidder Peabody & Co., Inc.
Barre W. Littel - Kidder Peabody & Co., Inc.
Patricia McConnell - Bear, Stearns & Company
William C. Norby - Duff and Phelps, Inc.
Thornton O'glove - Reporting Research Corporation
Charles A. Parker - The Continental Corporation
Lee Seidler - New York University
Gerald I. White - Grace & White, Inc.

These materials have been prepared by members of the technical staff of the FASB. Timothy S. Lucas, FASB project manager, is the primary author. The positions and opinions expressed are those of the author and not necessarily those of a majority of the task force or any individual task force member, or of the FASB or any Board member. Official positions of the FASB on accounting matters are determined only after extensive due process and deliberation.

Several other members of the technical staff also contributed their time, efforts, and ideas to this project, including Bryan Carsberg, Michael J. Cohen, Michael Fogg, Landa Miller, A. N. Phillips, and Beverly Welch. The author is indebted to Micheline S. Klucik and Vita M. Guglielmo for their assistance in editing and preparing successive drafts and to Linda W. Lapolla and John A. Pellegrino for transforming the final draft into a printed volume.

CONTENTS

PART I—AN INTRODUCTION TO INFLATION ACCOUNTING

PART II—MORE ABOUT INCOME, WITH ILLUSTRATIONS

PART I

An Introduction to Inflation Accounting

WHAT IS THIS BOOK ABOUT?

In brief, this book is about price changes and how they affect information in financial reports. The existence of significant rates of inflation in the U.S. economy is hardly news. Awareness of inflation, however, does not necessarily mean that people understand its effects. Inflation is a complex problem.

Inflation has been defined as an increase in the general level of prices and as a decrease in the value of the dollar. One of the complications is that prices of different items change at different rates. In fact, even when prices in general are rising, prices of some items may be declining. As a result, price changes do not affect all people or all companies equally.

Most people are generally aware that inflation affects the way they look at things. They know that a salary increase does not make them better off unless it exceeds the effects of inflation. They can give examples of ways in which inflation changes their behavior; for example, they may decide to borrow to buy things that they want in order to avoid anticipated price increases (especially if the effective after-tax interest rate is less than the inflation rate). They may be worried about saving for retirement; as time goes by, the purchasing power of their savings may diminish if interest rates are less than rates of inflation. As Alice told the Red Queen in *Through the Looking Glass*, they feel that they are running as fast as they can and hardly managing to stay in the same place.

A Fable for Our Times

Once upon a time, not very long ago and not very far away, there lived a young lad named Michael who liked candy bars. Every Saturday, Michael would use the last dime of his carefully budgeted allowance to purchase his favorite treat; but one day, he arrived at the corner store and found that candy bars had gone up to 15¢. "Darn," he said, "how can I get another nickel?"

Now Michael was an enterprising lad and decided to make his cash grow to meet his needs. Using the dime to purchase a lemon, he went into business as a lemonade merchant. He sold three glasses of lemonade for a nickel each. Happy with the return of his dime plus a 5¢ profit, he returned to the corner store only to discover that, while he had been hard at work, the price of the candy bar had increased to 20¢. Disappointed, but not discouraged, Michael decided to make his business a going concern. So he returned to the fruit counter, only to discover that the price of lemons had increased to 15¢. In order to continue in business, he would need to reinvest not only his original capital, but also all of his "profits."

We will consider Michael's story in more detail later, but first, fables are supposed to have a message that transcends the story's end. This fable has a dual, financial moral; changing prices affect everyone, including consumers and investors. Furthermore, when prices are changing, income or profit may not be what it seems at first glance.

Price changes cause problems, not only for lemonade merchants, but also for the largest businesses. A business must plan ahead to finance the replacement of inventory that is sold and plant and equipment that is being used up—expecting prices to be higher than when similar items were last purchased. Sometimes a business may wish to buy assets earlier than necessary so that it can avoid price increases. Investors and others who read financial reports need to know about the effects of inflation and how the business has reacted to them. Stockholders may evaluate business managers based on their ability to increase dividends and earnings by more than the rate of inflation; a dividend increase of 5 percent will not be considered good news if inflation is running at 10 percent. This book is about understanding the effects of changing prices on businesses and their financial statements.

WHAT DOES INFLATION HAVE TO DO WITH ACCOUNTING?

Accounting cannot stop or control inflation. The role of accounting is to communicate information about economic events—information that is useful in making business and economic decisions. If that information is inaccurate, incomplete, or not understood, decisions based on it may be adversely affected. If improved accounting information results in better decisions and more efficient allocation of resources, then improving the information may be part of the solution to overall economic problems such as inflation. Such macroeconomic benefits derived from the improved information would be in addition to the benefit of better decisions being made by the individual users of the information.

But is accounting information inaccurate, incomplete, or not understood because of inflation? Some believe so. Peter F. Drucker, in his recent book, *Managing in Turbulent Times,* wrote:

> . . . Executives today—both in businesses and in non-businesses and in non-business public service institutions—do not know the facts. What they think

---

*New York: Harper & Row, 1980, p. 10.

> are facts are largely illusions and half-truths. The reality
> of their enterprise is hidden, distorted and deformed
> by inflation. Executives today have available to them
> many times the reports, information, and figures their
> predecessors had; they have become dependent on
> these figures and are thus endangered if the figures lie
> to them. During inflation, however, the figures lie.
> Money still tends to be considered the standard of
> value and to be a value in itself, but in inflation this is
> delusion.

Not everyone agrees that the traditional accounting
figures "lie," but it is clear that, at best, they do not tell
the whole story and that additional information is
needed. This book is about that additional information
and the understanding that is critical to its usefulness.
Before we turn to an examination of this new information, however, it is helpful to review a few points about
traditional accounting statements.

The Starting Point:
Historical Cost Financial Statements

Traditional financial statements are prepared on a
historical cost basis. They summarize the transactions
of the business in terms of the actual—or nominal dollar*—prices. For example, when an asset is acquired.
the number of dollars paid is recorded in the company's books and that amount becomes the first
measure of the "book value" of the asset. Subsequent
increases in price or value are not recorded until the
asset is sold or exchanged, perhaps years later. At the
time of a sale, income is measured by subtracting the

---

*The term *nominal dollars* is used to refer to amounts
expressed in actual dollars to differentiate them from *constant dollars*. An amount expressed in *constant dollars* has
been adjusted to reflect the purchasing power of the dollar at
a specific time. Amounts in *nominal dollars* are not so
adjusted.

original cost of the asset from the proceeds of the sale. Some assets (for example, factories) are purchased for use in the business. Part of the cost of such assets is systematically written off each year as depreciation expense so that the book value of the asset is steadily reduced. This process reflects the "using up" or "expiration" of the asset.

When prices change rapidly, the historical cost approach does not provide all needed information about business performance. If an asset has been held for a long time, income (measured as the difference between selling price and original cost), may appear to be large. However, such a computation overlooks the fact that each dollar of the selling price is worth less (has a lower purchasing power) than each dollar of the original cost. Also, if the company chooses to replace an asset, it may find that a significant portion of its traditional "income" must be reinvested, because the price of the asset has risen. Neither of these considerations is reported in the traditional historical cost statements. Further limitations of the traditional system are apparent when amounts measured at different dates are compared. An investor who receives a dividend of $1.00 in 1979 and $1.05 in 1980 has received increased nominal dollars. In spite of this upward trend, however, the $1.05 in 1980 will not buy as much, on average, as the 1979 dividend bought.

Most people agree that the information contained in historical cost financial statements is reliable, verifiable, and useful. Most people also believe that additional information is needed during periods of significant changes in prices.

WHAT HAS THE FASB DONE ABOUT IT?

In September 1979, the Financial Accounting Standards Board made a significant move toward meeting the need when it issued FASB Statement No. 33, *Financial Reporting and Changing Prices.* Statement 33 requires that information about the effects of inflation and specific price changes on corporate operations be included in the annual reports of large corporations. Basic financial statements prepared under the historical cost method have not changed; rather, the adjusted data is supplementary. Two kinds of supplementary information are provided. One focuses on adjustments for inflation or changes in the general level of prices. That information is known as *constant dollar* information (or strictly speaking, *historical cost/constant dollar* information). The other type of information reflects the prices of specific goods and services that a business buys and uses and is known as *current cost* information.

Statement 33 does not require presentation of a complete set of financial statements adjusted for all the effects of changing prices. It requires supplemental computations of operating income, incorporating

---

The Statement explicitly encourages experimentation.

---

adjustments of cost of goods sold and depreciation and amortization expenses, and certain other "free-standing" information. It also requires a five-year summary of key information. It does not require a supplementary balance sheet. However, some businesses may elect to provide more than the required minimum. In addition, managers must explain the meaning of the new information and interpret its significance in terms of the business of the company.

The Statement applies to all public companies that have either total assets of more than $1 billion or inventories and gross property, plant, and equipment of more than $125 million at the beginning of the year. The Statement explicitly encourages experimentation. The new requirements have been actively debated and carefully decided, but perceptions may change with experience and improvements may emerge. Companies are encouraged to strive for the clearest ways to communicate the impact of changing prices on their operations. As experience is gained, the FASB, working with the business community (including people who *use* financial information), will gather evidence about the usefulness of the information and will be prepared to revise the Statement.

WHAT IS CONSTANT DOLLAR INFORMATION?

Constant dollar information is a result of adjusting the numbers in the basic financial statements for changes in the general level of prices. The result is an expression of the financial information in terms of a different measuring unit: dollars of equal purchasing power or *constant dollars*.

Why is a new measuring unit needed? The desirability of a new measuring unit is illustrated by an example from outside of accounting. Assume that we want to know the length of a football field. We take a yardstick and start measuring the field. Suppose, however, that after each 5 yards someone shortens our yardstick by 1 inch; it would then be only 17 inches long by the time we reach the other goal. If we express our measurement in "yardsticks," it will be of little use. The size of the unit of measure changed during the measuring process.

Even with a shrinking yardstick it is possible to measure the field. But we must decide on the unit of measure to be used. We can use the original 36-inch yard as the unit and report that the field is 100 yards long. Or we can use "ending yards," which are 17 inches long, and report that the field is 212 "yards" long. Of course, the real length of the field has not changed and we would not want to imply that the field "grew" by 112 yards during our experiment.

When the purchasing power of the dollar changes over time, a similar difficulty arises. Each dollar of a 1978 expenditure of $100 has a different purchasing power from each dollar of a 1979 receipt of $140. Yet such differences in the measuring unit are ignored in traditional accounting. If an item purchased for $100 in 1978 is sold for $140 in 1979, we compute profit of $40. Some people suggest that is like subtracting two yards from six feet; the arithmetic answer of four is not useful. Only if the measurements were adjusted, so that, for example, the expenditure was expressed as $111 in dollars with 1979 purchasing power, would a constant dollar measuring unit have been used. Because constant dollar information is expressed in units of constant "size," the resulting figures may be added, subtracted, and compared without making subjective allowances or ad hoc corrections for inflation.

It is easy to understand the need for a constant unit with which to measure length. A constant unit is required to mark out equal distances in different locations or to determine whether one distance is longer than another and by how much. The same need is apparent for other physical measurements, such as weight. The need for constant units in financial measurements may be less obvious. Constant units allow us to assess the significance of price changes over time. For example, in 1975 a car might have cost

$3,500; a comparable 1980 model might be priced at $5,000. If a car buyer calculates the 1980 purchasing power of the 3,500 1975 dollars, a new perspective on the apparent price increase results. The 3,500 1975 dollars are approximately equal in purchasing power to 5,359 1980 dollars. If the consumer's income has increased with the inflation rate, the percentage of

---

Statement 33 requires the use of the Consumer Price Index.

---

income required to purchase a new car has actually decreased.

Statement 33 requires the use of the Consumer Price Index for All Urban Consumers (CPI) to fix the size of a constant dollar. That index, published each month by the Bureau of Labor Statistics, measures the level of inflation by comparing past and present costs of purchasing a particular group of goods and services selected to represent a typical pattern of personal spending. In 1967, the base year, the index has a value of 100; in 1980 (on average) the index stood at 247. In other words, it took $2.47 in 1980 to equal the purchasing power of $1.00 in 1967.

We noted above that the impact of inflation varies as the prices of different items increase at different rates. If John buys only bread and Linda buys only meat and the price of meat increases while the price of bread remains constant, then inflation has affected Linda more than John. As a result, any measure of overall inflation must be some kind of an average of price changes on particular goods and services. In other words, the purchasing power of the dollar cannot be calculated exactly; it can only be estimated on an average basis.

The CPI is computed based on a specific "market basket" of items typically purchased by urban consumers. Other indexes, using different "market baskets" of goods and services, will show rates of inflation somewhat different from the CPI. Some people have suggested that other indexes, such as the gross national product deflator, should be used to adjust financial data because they are more representative of what companies buy. Others have argued that the CPI is based on the wrong "market basket" of goods—for example, that it includes too much housing. Overall, however, the CPI is probably a reasonable approximation of the average purchasing power of the dollar and that is what investors are interested in. It also has some practical advantages in that it is issued monthly without a long delay and is not often revised.

WHAT IS CURRENT COST?

Current cost is the cost of an item today, as opposed to historical cost, which is the cost of the item at the time it was purchased. Current cost accounting deducts the current cost of assets sold or used up from revenues to measure operating income. The prices used in calculating current cost operating income are specific prices of the specific items sold or used during the current period, rather than an average of a "market basket" of other goods and services. Specific prices change as a result of a variety of factors, such as changes in the cost of production (perhaps as a result of technological improvements) or changes in demand (perhaps the result of changes in consumers' taste).

The relevance of measurements of current cost may be illustrated by a simple example. Suppose that a neighbor has run out of cooking oil and asks to borrow some. You have an unopened bottle of oil which you purchased last week for $2.60, although the price has since increased to $2.95. Your neighbor insists on paying you. What would be a fair price? You know that you will be going to the supermarket in the next few days and could pick up a bottle of cooking oil without inconvenience. You conclude that $2.95 would be a fair price because, with that amount of money, you can get back to the position you were in before helping out your neighbor. The original cost of the bottle you gave the neighbor is irrelevant because it is no longer enough to buy a bottle of oil.

In most cases, as with the cooking oil, the current cost of an asset is the cost to replace it. A business that sells an asset for $1.00, and then replaces it by paying $1.10 for an identical asset, would have been better off if it had just held on to the original asset. Or, it may decide to sell the asset and not replace it. In general, if a business intends to replace an asset, it will not want to sell or use the asset unless it receives more than the *current cost* in return. Current cost income is the amount by which revenues exceed the cost of replacing the items sold or used to produce the revenues. In other words, it is the amount left over after the business has been restored to the position it was in before making the sale.

The idea of current cost is relatively easy to grasp for inventory which is sold and then is likely to be replaced. It is more difficult for assets, such as a factory, that are used over a long period and are not replaced each period. Part of the difficulty results from our inability to measure how much of the factory was actually used up in a particular year. The current cost approach, like the traditional historical cost financial statements, uses a systematic depreciation method to reflect (approximately) the "using up" of such assets. The difference is that the depreciation method is applied to the current cost of assets rather than to their historical cost.

Sometimes a business will not want to replace a particular kind of asset because it has become obsolete or no one wants to buy the output it produces. In that case, the value to the business of the asset will have become small—the firm would not be willing to pay very much to acquire the asset if it did not already own it. The amount the company would accept for the sale of the asset will be similarly small. Current cost accounting recognizes those circumstances; the

---

The measurement rule is current cost or lower recoverable amount.

---

measurement is limited to the amount expected to be recovered by using or selling the asset. Hence, the measurement rule in current cost accounting is *current cost or lower recoverable amount.*

Current cost measurements may provide useful information about assets that are held by a business as well as those that are used or sold. If the current cost (that is, the specific price) of an asset has increased, it may be because the asset can be used to earn more than previously and, therefore, people are willing to pay more for it. Thus, increases in the current cost of assets held by a company may provide a clue to the increases in the cash flows and earnings that the assets will be able to generate in the future. That is a general, rather than an exact, relationship, however, and as a result, information on current costs must be used with caution. It is likely to be a better basis for assessing future cash flows than historical cost information but it must be interpreted with an appreciation of the economics of the industry in which the business concerned operates.

Current costs are measured at the dates of use or sale of the assets concerned. If expenses measured at current cost are deducted from revenues to determine income, both revenues and expenses are automatically measured in dollars of the same purchasing power. No constant dollar adjustments are required. If, however, we want to make a comparison between current cost amounts for this year and for last year, dollars of different sizes are involved. To improve comparisons of information for different years, current cost amounts for prior years can be adjusted to a constant dollar basis using a general price index as described above for constant dollar accounting.

HOW DO BUSINESSES DETERMINE CURRENT COST?

Estimates or measurements of current cost can be obtained in a variety of ways.

- Direct Pricing: Companies may estimate current cost on the basis of invoice prices, vendor price lists, or quotations provided by suppliers.
- Indexation: Companies may calculate the current cost of an asset by multiplying its historical cost by the change in a specific price index. The selected index would be specific to the types of assets involved and not a general price index such as the CPI. For example, an index of construction costs might be used to estimate the current cost of a building.
- Unit Pricing: This method might be used, for example, to determine the current value of a building. The company might select an appropriate unit—square feet of building space, perhaps—and estimate the current cost of the building based on current engineering estimates

of cost per square foot of similar buildings.

- Functional Pricing: Instead of estimating the current cost of the actual asset owned, the company might estimate the cost of a newer asset that performs the same function and adjust that cost for any advantage of the newer asset, such as the fact that it reduces the amount of raw material used.

As these methods indicate, the measurement of current cost involves estimates and requires new approaches. One of the goals of the Statement 33 experiment is to gain experience with such measurements and learn about their usefulness.

DOESN'T LIFO ADJUST THE FINANCIAL STATEMENTS FOR INFLATION?

Statement 33 requires disclosure of certain items on a current cost basis, including cost of goods sold, depreciation, inventory, and property, plant, and equipment. The differences between these numbers and the corresponding items in the basic financial statements will depend partly on the choice of accounting methods applied in preparing the basic statements. In some cases, those methods used are, in effect, partially adjusted for inflation.

Two common methods for measuring cost of goods sold and inventory are FIFO (first-in, first-out) and LIFO (last-in, first-out). Cost of goods sold in the basic financial statements will normally approximate the current cost of goods sold for a business that uses LIFO. Suppose a business buys and sells 100 widgets per month and that its inventory is constant at 200 widgets. The price of widgets was $8 when the business first purchased them and increased to $10 on January 1,

1980 and remained at that level. Cost of goods sold and inventory measurements for the calendar year 1980 are as follows:

| | Basic Financial Statements | | Current Cost |
	FIFO	LIFO	
Cost of goods sold	(2 x 100 x $8) + (10 x 100 x $10) = $11,600	12 x100 x$10 = $12,000	$12,000
Inventory at year-end	200 x $10 = $2,000	200 x $8 = $1,600	$ 2,000

Under FIFO, the goods purchased in November and December at $8 per unit are assumed to be sold in January and February; under LIFO, the $8 goods are assumed to be retained in inventory and the units sold are assumed to be those most recently purchased. Although LIFO generally produces an "up-to-date" measure of cost of goods sold, it produces an "out-of-date" measure of inventory at year-end. Results may also be affected by decreases in inventory in some periods (that is, "LIFO layer invasions"). The current cost system measures both cost of goods sold and inventory on a current cost or "up-to-date" basis.

Some businesses have computed depreciation expense in the basic financial statements by using an accelerated method of depreciation. Accelerated depreciation means higher depreciation expense in the early years of an asset's life and correspondingly lower depreciation expense in the later years of an asset's life. The result can be somewhat similar to the effect of the use of LIFO. Expenses are recognized sooner but the net asset measurement (original cost less depreciation) is reduced. The extent to which accelerated depreciation in the primary statements gives an approximation of current cost depreciation expense will depend on the pattern of acquisition of assets and other factors.

WHAT IS INCOME?

Most people have an intuitive idea of what income is. For an individual who receives a salary, the measurement of income presents few problems. The salary, perhaps reduced by any job-related expenses incurred by the employee, is *income*. For a company that buys raw materials or inventory and sells products, the measurement of what we intuitively think of as income is more difficult. The sales proceeds (revenues) must be reduced by the cost of acquiring or producing the goods that were sold. In other words, *income* is the excess of revenues over the amounts expended to produce the revenues. It is also how much more the business has—how much better off it is—at the end of the period. When prices change, however, the simple concept of *income* becomes difficult to apply.

Part II of this book discusses the idea of income in more detail. The remainder of Part I discusses the meaning and use of the information required by Statement 33, including information about income.

The Fable Revisited

At the beginning of this book, we introduced "A Fable for Our Times," the story of Michael and his lemonade venture. That simple story may be used to illustrate how the intuitive idea of income is complicated when prices are changing.

Michael paid 10¢ for a lemon and recorded sales of lemonade totaling 15¢. One measure of his income (corresponding to the historical cost approach used in the primary financial statements) is 5¢.

When Michael returned to the store to buy another lemon, however, the cost of his raw material had increased to 15¢. Another possible income measure (corresponding to current cost operating income) is the difference between revenues and the cost that would be required to replace the raw material used so that the business could continue. Michael's income on that basis is zero. This is particularly relevant if he decides to continue in the lemonade business by replacing the lemon.

Michael's objective in entering the lemonade business was to purchase a candy bar that cost 15¢ at the time he started his business. Viewing income in terms of progress toward that goal, a third computation of income is possible. In the beginning, Michael had 10¢ and a candy bar cost 15¢, so he had purchasing power equal to 67% of a candy bar. At the end of the period, he had 15¢ equal to 75% of a 20¢ candy bar. His progress toward his goal might be expressed as 8% of a bar (75% - 67%). If the CPI increased at the same rate as the price of candy bars, this would correspond to operating income based on the constant dollar approach of 1.6¢ (8% of 20¢) in end-of-period cents. Michael's *purchasing power* increased by that much. Of course, the computation is a little more complicated if there is more than one consumer good to consider.

So Michael's income over the period of the tale is ambiguous; it depends on the perspective from which we view it. Statement 33 is intended to provide users of financial reports with information that will enable them to assess income from several different viewpoints.

WHAT DOES THE NEW INFORMATION LOOK LIKE?

Because of the experimental nature of the Statement and the flexibility it allows, the format of the information varies from one company to another. In general, however, the new information is presented in three parts:

- Supplementary measures of operating income and related information
- A five-year summary of key information adjusted for inflation, including sales, dividends, stock prices, and measures of income and net assets
- A narrative section prepared by management explaining the meaning of the new information and the impact of inflation on the company

A simplified example illustrating the preparation of the information is presented in Part II of this book. A realistic example of what the new information looks like appears on pages 22 and 23. Two examples of actual disclosures, including the management's discussion portion, are reproduced beginning on page 40.

Schedule A gives information for the current year. The main part of the schedule contains information on income; it presents a summary of the operating income computation in the basic financial statements for comparative purposes and then shows corresponding computations on a constant dollar basis (middle column) and on a current cost basis. If you examine each row, you will see that four line items—sales, other operating expense, interest expense, and provision for income taxes—are the same in all columns. The presentation conforms to the minimum requirements of Statement 33. Only cost of goods sold and depreciation and amortization expense are adjusted because these adjustments are the ones likely to have the biggest impact on income.

Adjustments to other items are likely to be less significant in their effect on income. The additional adjustments, resulting in what is called "comprehensive restatement," may be made at the option of the company's management. The bottom line of the computations is called *income from continuing operations.* Statement 33 does not require presentation of information on extraordinary items, discontinued operations, or prior-year adjustments.

Now consider the numbers in Schedule A for cost of goods sold and depreciation and amortization expense. In both cases, the constant dollar numbers are higher than the historical cost numbers. This normally will be the case in times of inflation because the constant dollar numbers are obtained by adjusting historical cost by the change in the consumer price index between the date of acquisition of the resources and the date of use or sale. The current cost numbers may be higher or lower than the constant dollar numbers because the prices of resources used in the business may change more or less than prices in general.

Linked with the information on income are two free-standing items: the gain (or loss) from the change in purchasing power of monetary items and the increase (or decrease) in the current cost of inventory and property, plant, and equipment (often called *holding gain or loss*). The first of these items is presented for consideration in relation to both constant dollar information and current cost information; the second relates only to current cost information. Neither has a direct counterpart in the basic statements. The significance of these items is described later in this book.

Schedule A

MANUFACTURING COMPANY ILLUSTRATION
SCHEDULE OF INCOME FROM CONTINUING OPERATIONS
ADJUSTED FOR CHANGING PRICES
For the Year Ended December 31, 19X5
(In Millions of Dollars)

	As Reported in the Financial Statements (Historical Cost)	Adjusted for General Inflation (Constant Dollar)	Adjusted for Changes in Specific Prices (Current Cost)
Sales	$10,081	$10,081	$10,081
Cost of goods sold	8,161	8,179	8,190
Depreciation and amortization expense	483	551	620
Other operating expense	329	329	329
Interest expense	57	57	57
Provision for income taxes (a)	491	491	491
	9,521	9,607	9,687
Income from continuing operations	$ 560	$ 474	$ 394
Per share	$ 1.91	$ 1.62	$ 1.34
Gain from decline in purchasing power of net amounts owed		$ 11	$ 11
Increase in current costs of inventories and property, plant, and equipment:			
Total (nominal dollar) increase			$ 1,087
Increase due to general inflation			234
Increase net of effects of general inflation			$ 853

(a) In accordance with Statement 33, no adjustment has been made to the provision for income taxes.

(b) At December 31, 19X5, current cost of inventory was $1,381 and current cost of property, plant, and equipment, net of accumulated depreciation, was $2,756. The current cost of property owned and the related depreciation expense were calculated by applying selected wholesale price indexes to historical book values.

Schedule B

**MANUFACTURING COMPANY ILLUSTRATION
COMPARISON OF SELECTED DATA
ADJUSTED FOR EFFECTS OF CHANGING PRICES
($ in Millions Except per Share Amounts)**

	19X5	19X4	19X3	19X2	19X1
Sales - as reported	$10,081	$8,791	$7,543	$5,689	$5,021
- in constant dollars (a)	$10,081	$9,464	$8,645	$6,896	$6,643
Income from operations					
- as reported	$ 560	$ 529	$ 460	$ 197	$ 149
- based on constant dollars (a)	$ 474	$ 500	$ 458	$ 63	$ 30
- based on current cost (a)	$ 394	$ 410	$ 391	$ 82	$ 66
Income from operations per share					
- as reported	$ 1.91	$ 1.81	$ 1.57	$ .67	$ .51
- in constant dollars (a)	$ 1.62	$ 1.71	$ 1.56	$ .22	$ .10
- in current cost (a)	$ 1.34	$ 1.40	$ 1.33	$ .28	$ .23
Common stock dividends per share					
- as reported	$ 1.06	$ 1.06	$ .89	$ .38	$ .54
- in constant dollars (a)	$ 1.06	$ 1.14	$ 1.02	$ .46	$ .71
Net assets at year-end					
- as reported	$ 2,796	$2,508	$2,288	$2,082	$1,994
- in constant dollars (a)	$ 3,600	$3,500	$3,400	$3,300	$3,200
- in current cost (a)	$ 4,500	$4,300	$4,100	$4,000	$3,800
Increase in specific prices of inventory and property over increase in general price level - net (a)	$ 853	$ 769	$ 693	$ 611	$ 505
Gain from decline in purchasing power of net amounts owed (a)	$ 11	$ 13	$ 8	$ 6	$ 3
Market price per common share at year-end (a)	$ 9	$ 11	$ 14	$ 11	$ 7
Average consumer price index	195.4	181.5	170.5	161.2	147.7

(a) In average 19X5 dollars.

Schedule B presents a five-year summary of selected financial information. All columns in the schedule are reported in constant (average 19X5) dollars. This means that the numbers will differ from those previously reported. For example, in the 19X5 report illustrated (Schedule B), sales for the year 19X4 are shown as $9,464. That amount (like all amounts in the table) is expressed in average 19X5 dollars and, therefore, would be different from 19X4 sales as previously reported in the 19X4 report ($8,791). Based on the CPI, $9,464 in 19X5 had the same purchasing power as $8,791 in 19X4. The numbers are adjusted to reflect the same amount of purchasing power in different units. Consequently, trends shown in the five-year summary are after adjustment for general inflation; for example, an increase in sales will be shown only if sales, in nominal dollars, increased faster than the general price level. This process of adjusting trends for inflation is the same as that used in presenting macroeconomic data. When we read in the paper that "real gross national product increased 2% last year" or "real personal income declined by 1% last year" we are dealing with amounts adjusted for inflation. The term *real* is used in economics to indicate that a trend has been expressed in constant dollars.

Individual businesses have flexibility in the manner in which they present the information required by Statement 33. It is hoped that businesses will experiment to help identify the most useful formats. Some businesses may elect not to present the current-year information in columns; they may prefer a format that reconciles income reported in the basic statements to constant dollar income and current cost income. Similarly, disclosure of historical cost information beside the new information is not required, even if a columnar format is chosen.

WHAT DO THE NEW NUMBERS MEAN?

Information about Performance

The primary focus of the new information is on information about performance. It calls for four main building blocks:

- Constant dollar income from continuing operations
- Current cost income from continuing operations
- Increase or decrease in prices of inventories and property, plant, and equipment (often called *holding gains* or *holding losses*)
- Purchasing power gain or loss on net monetary items

The meaning and usefulness of these and other Statement 33 disclosures are discussed in the following sections. In general, the new information about performance will be used in the same ways and for the same purposes as traditional information. In fact, if there were no price changes at all, income from continuing operations would be exactly the same amount on current cost, constant dollar, and historical cost bases.

For convenience, in the rest of this book we will refer to the four principal components of the Statement 33 information by the following short titles:

- Constant dollar operating income
- Current cost operating income
- Holding gain or loss (nominal or net)
- Monetary gain or loss

The holding gain or loss is required to be reported both before (nominal) and after (net) deducting the effects of general inflation.

Constant Dollar Income from Continuing Operations

Constant dollar operating income is the difference between the purchasing power of revenues and the purchasing power sacrificed to acquire the goods that have been sold. The accounting principles used are similar to traditional historical cost principles. However, cost of goods sold and depreciation expense are restated to reflect the rate of inflation between the acquisition of the related assets and their date of use or sale. In other words, they are restated to show the number of today's nominal dollars that would be needed to have the same purchasing power as the dollars spent to acquire the assets. Constant dollar operating income would be the same as historical cost income if the purchasing power of the dollar were unchanged—if there were no inflation.

Current Cost Income from Continuing Operations

Current cost operating income is the difference between revenues and the current cost of producing or buying the goods that have been sold. The difference between current cost operating income and historical cost income results from adjustments to cost of goods sold and depreciation expense to reflect specific prices at the dates assets are used or sold.

Current cost operating income is often linked to a concept called *distributable income*—the amount that the company could distribute as dividends without reducing its physical holdings of inventory and property, plant, and equipment. In a simplified case, such as those considered in this book (for example, the Blouse Company case on page 33), it is easy to see that current cost operating income is the amount the company has left over after providing for the current cost of replacing items sold or used—that is, after maintaining the company's ability to sell or produce or operate at the same level in the future.

In a real-world situation, there are several reasons why current cost operating income is no more than an approximation of, or a guide to, distributable income. For example, the company may need to increase receivables to support a higher level of nominal dollar sales or it may be able to borrow to finance replacement of assets sold or used.* In spite of these limitations, the *distributable income* idea may be helpful in understanding current cost operating income.

Comparison of Constant Dollar and Current Cost

A simple example may illustrate the difference between the constant dollar and current cost approaches to calculating income from continuing operations. The Fork Co. bought an item on January 1 for $1.00. On June 30, it sold the item for $2.00 and purchased a replacement item for $1.20. The CPI was 100 on January 1 and 110 on June 30. The average level of the CPI during the calendar year was also 110. On a constant dollar basis (using average-for-the-year dollars as the measuring unit), the company would compute the purchasing power of the $1.00 spent on January 1. Cost of sales would be adjusted to this amount ($1.10), revenues would be unchanged because they are already expressed in average-for-the-year dollars, and constant dollar operating income would be $.90.

On a current cost basis, the company would measure cost of sales at the current cost of the item sold ($1.20)

---

*Paragraphs 124-130 of Statement 33 discuss the *distributable income* concept and its limitations in more detail.

and would report current cost operating income of
$.80. In that case, no further adjustment is required to
express the numbers in constant dollars. Cost of sales
is measured at the date of sale and, consequently, both
sales and cost of sales are measured in dollars having
the same purchasing power.

Table 1
THE FORK CO.

	Historical Cost	Constant Dollar	Current Cost
Sales	$2.00	$2.00	$2.00
Cost of sales	1.00	1.10	1.20
Income from operations	$1.00	$ .90	$ .80

Table 1 sets out three measures of income from continuing operations for this simple example. They are
$1.00, $.90, and $.80 and each represents the com-
pany's income from a different perspective. Comparison of the different numbers helps to explain
effects of price changes on a company.

Changes in Prices of Inventories and Property, Plant, and Equipment Held

Changes in the current costs of inventories, property,
plant, and equipment while they are held awaiting use
or sale are often called *holding gains* or *holding losses*.
They arise under the current cost approach. In the Fork
Co. example above, in addition to current cost operating income of $.80, the company would have a
nominal holding gain of $.20 because the current cost
of the inventory item increased from $1.00 to $1.20
while the company held it. Of the $.20 holding gain, it
may be said the $.10 corresponds to (or represents the
effect of) general inflation of 10% and the remaining
$.10 represents a holding gain net of inflation, some-
times referred to as a "real" holding gain or a constant
dollar holding gain.

Current cost operating income may be differentiated from holding gains and losses by describing the former as income from selling goods for more than their current cost and the latter as a gain from holding goods during a period when the price of the goods increases. Suppose that the Fork Co. had not sold the item (purchased for $1.00) but continued to hold it until year-end, when the price of the item was $1.25. The company would have no revenue and no current cost operating income but it would have a holding gain (in nominal dollar terms) of $.25. If inflation for the full year was 15%, $.15 of that could be said to represent the effect of general inflation. The holding gain adjusted for inflation, or *net holding gain*, of $.10 indicates that the price of this asset increased by more than the general price level.

If the company held a second asset priced at $2.00 on January 1 and $2.10 on December 31, the nominal holding gain would be $.10 and the effect of inflation would be $.30, resulting in a net holding loss of $.20. The net holding loss indicates that the price of the second asset increased less than the general price level. Table 2 summarizes this example for both assets.

Table 2
THE FORK CO.

	Asset 1	Asset 2
Price at December 31	$1.25	$2.10
Price at January 1	1.00	2.00
Nominal holding gain	.25	.10
Effect of general price level increase (15%)	.15	.30
Net holding gain (loss)	$ .10	$(.20)

Statement 33 requires the disclosure of holding gains and losses both before and after adjusting for the effect of general inflation. However, it does not use the terms *holding gain* and *holding loss.* It refers instead to *increases and decreases in current cost amounts* because there is controversy about the relationship between "holding gains" and income. Some interpret holding gains as favorable since they mean that the company owns something that has increased in value and is, therefore, better off. Holding gains may also

---

There is controversy about the relationship between "holding gains" and income.

---

reflect cost savings from buying items before they were used or sold, thereby reducing costs by the amount of price increases occurring subsequently. On the other hand, increases in the current costs of the things a company buys indicate that, when items on hand are used, replacements will cost more. There is no guarantee that the company will be able to raise prices enough to cover the resulting cost increases and maintain its profit margins. Pricing flexibility may be limited, for example, by competitive conditions. In this view, "holding gains" are unfavorable, representing cost increases.

Holding gains (or losses) may be either *realized*— meaning that the asset has been sold or used—or they may be *unrealized*—meaning that the asset is still held by the company. *Realized* holding gains are included in operating income in the basic (historical cost) financial statements but they are not shown separately. These gains include what are often called *inventory profits.* *Unrealized* holding gains are not reflected or included in the traditional income statement. Further, the *realized* holding gains that are included are those realized in the current period, without regard to whether they result from price changes in the current period or price changes that occurred in any of the earlier periods while the asset was held. Holding losses are generally treated similarly, except that some *unrealized* holding losses may be recognized (for example, through use of lower of cost or market rules).

The relationship between realized holding gains and traditional historical cost net income may be clarified by looking again at the Fork Co. example on page 28. In the first situation described, where the item purchased for $1.00 was sold for $2.00 at a time when its current cost was $1.20, there was a $.20 nominal holding gain. Since that gain was *realized* when the item was sold, the $.20 is included in the $1.00 historical cost operating income shown in Table 1. In the second situation, where the Fork Co. is assumed to hold the item instead of selling it, the gain was *unrealized* and was not included in operating income.

Under current cost accounting in Statement 33, realized and unrealized holding gains and losses that result from changes in the current period in prices of inventory and property, plant, and equipment are reported as *increases and decreases in current cost amounts*. Holding gains or losses are generally excluded from operating income.

Gain or Loss in Purchasing Power on Net Monetary Items

This component may be described in various ways, such as *gain from decline in purchasing power of net amounts owed* or *loss from decline in purchasing power of net monetary assets held*. In this book we will refer to it simply as the *monetary gain or loss*; it is a measure of the effect of holding monetary assets or liabilities.

Monetary assets include cash and claims to receive a

fixed amount of money (such as receivables). Holders of monetary assets experience a loss of purchasing power due to inflation because the amount of goods and services that can be bought with a fixed sum is reduced by inflation. Monetary liabilities are obligations to pay fixed amounts of money in the future. A borrower experiences a gain from inflation because the fixed amount of money required to repay the loan diminishes in purchasing power. A brief example illustrates this point. Suppose that a company holds cash of $1.00 throughout a year while the CPI increases by 10%; that dollar will buy less at year-end than it would have bought on January 1. A 10% increase in the CPI indicates that it would take $1.10 at year-end to match the purchasing power of the original $1.00. Therefore, the company lost $.10 worth of purchasing power, measured in end-of-year dollars.

Companies that have more monetary assets than liabilities will show a net loss of purchasing power when there is inflation. If deflation occurred—if the general level of prices fell—they would have a gain. A majority of nonfinancial companies (that is, excluding banks, insurance companies, etc.) have more monetary liabilities than assets. In times of inflation such companies show a net gain in purchasing power, reflecting the fact that they will be able to repay with dollars of reduced purchasing power. Some have suggested that the monetary gain (or loss) is really an adjustment to interest expense (or revenue), since lenders generally compensate for expected inflation by raising interest rates. In this view, the sum of nominal interest and the monetary gain or loss is interest adjusted for inflation or "real" interest. Since nominal interest is a component of operating income, those who hold this view may wish to add the monetary gain or loss to operating income to determine overall results or to measure performance.

An Illustration

Constant dollar information, based on a general index of the purchasing power of the dollar, provides information about whether a business is receiving more purchasing power in the form of revenues than it is paying out or using up to produce those revenues. The added purchasing power acquired (or earned) in this way may be distributed as dividends, or it may be reinvested by the business to earn further returns.

It is often said that the current cost approach better measures the impact of changing prices *on a business* because it is based on the prices of things the business buys. This is particularly true if the company continues in the same business. Constant dollar information, however, may be particularly relevant to the investor who is interested in receiving a return on investment in terms of purchasing power or for the company that engages in changing lines of business. In other words, both current cost and constant dollar information, as well as comparisons between them, will provide useful information.

At this point, a simple example may help to illustrate how both current cost information and constant dollar information provide insights into a company's performance when prices are changing. The Blouse Company is a wholesaler of clothing. It begins operations in year 1 with $1,000 of capital which is invested in inventory to be sold at cost plus 10%. The same physical amount of inventory is purchased each year on January 1 and sold on December 31. Current costs of Blouse's products increase at 10% per year. The general price level, however, increases at 25%. The company is assumed to liquidate. at the end of year 3. Blouse's summarized transactions are shown in Table 3.

Table 3
BLOUSE COMPANY

	Purchases	Sales	Historical Cost Operating Income	CPI at 1/1	CPI at 12/31
Year 1	$1,000	$1,100	$100	100.00	125.00
Year 2	$1,100	$1,210	110	125.00	156.25
Year 3	$1,210	$1,331	121	156.25	195.31
			$ 331		

Supplemental current cost and constant dollar information may be computed as shown in Tables 4 and 5. Because the price of inventory items increases at 10%, and the company's markup is also 10%, current cost operating income is zero in each year. Because the general price level increases at a higher rate (25%), the company experiences inventory holding losses on a net of inflation basis.

Table 4
BLOUSE COMPANY
Current Cost Information
(In Nominal Dollars)

	Sales	Cost of Sales	Operating Income	Nominal Holding Gain	Net Holding Gain (Loss) in 12/31/3 Dollars*
Year 1	$1,100	$1,100	$0	$100	$(234)
Year 2	$1,210	$1,210	$0	110	(204)
Year 3	$1,331	$1,331	$0	121	(181)
				$331	$(619)

*The net holding gain is actually a constant dollar concept and is, therefore, expressed in end-of-year-3 constant dollars rather than nominal dollars.

Table 5
BLOUSE COMPANY
Constant Dollar Information
(In 12/31/3 Dollars)

	Sales	Cost of Sales	Operating Income (Loss)
Year 1	$1,716	$1,950	$(234)
Year 2	$1,512	$1,716	(204)
Year 3	$1,331	$1,512	(181)
			$(619)

The constant dollar information shows that Blouse Company has lost purchasing power totaling 619 end-of-year-3 dollars. At the end of year 3, a liquidating dividend of $1,331 will buy the stockholders less than the original $1,000 (1,950 end-of-year-3 dollars) would have bought. In other words, the stockholders would have had to receive $1,950 at the end of year 3 in order to have purchasing power equal to the $1000 invested in year 1.

Combinations

The individual measures of performance provided for in Statement 33 may also be combined by those who use the information to obtain additional, more comprehensive, information. Some of the more interesting combinations are described below.

Constant Dollar Operating Income + Monetary Gain or Loss

The two components that are based on the constant dollar approach may be logically added together. The sum of constant dollar operating income and the monetary gain or loss may be thought of as the increase in the company's net assets measured at cost

in units of constant purchasing power.* Combining
these two components is also appropriate if the monetary gain or loss is viewed as an adjustment to nominal
interest rates.

Current Cost Operating Income
+ Nominal Holding Gain

The combination of the two exclusively current cost
components may be thought of as the increase during
the current year in the company's net assets measured
at current cost.* It includes the total effect of increases
in the prices of assets held without any adjustment for
general inflation. The combined measure may be useful
as an indicator of overall performance on a current cost
basis.

Current Cost Operating Income
+ Net Holding Gains and Losses
+ Monetary Gain or Loss

A third aggregation combines the current cost and
constant dollar perspectives. It represents the increase
in net assets measured at current cost,* but excludes
increases that reflect the amount of general inflation
during the period. It is the most comprehensive of the
performance measures discussed here. It may be
thought of as the increase in the current cost of net
assets expressed in units of constant purchasing
power.* As such, it might be described as the "real"
increase in net assets measured at current cost.

---

*Other factors that change net assets, but are not part of the
income measures described, include dividends, additional
investments by owners, extraordinary items, and results of
discontinued operations.

Information about Assets

Statement 33 requires information about the amount of the company's net assets based on constant dollar and current cost approaches. That information may be useful alone or in combination with the new income information.

Constant dollar net asset amounts, like other constant dollar components, are computed using the CPI as an indicator of the change in purchasing power of the dollar. Only inventories and fixed assets (including land) are required to be adjusted, and the reported amounts are computed after depreciation has been deducted. All other assets and liabilities are presented at the original historical cost amounts (in nominal dollars).

Like constant dollar, the current cost net asset amount adjusts only inventories and fixed assets. The adjustments are based on estimates of the current prices of the assets. While this probably is not the amount the company could receive if it sold the assets,* many people feel it provides the best reflection of the capacity of the company's assets to generate future cash flows because it reflects what it would cost to acquire the assets at current prices or their value to the business if that is lower.

Trends

Statement 33 requires disclosure of sales, dividends, year-end stock prices, and the information about per-

---

*Selling prices available to a company depend on the circumstances of sale and the market in which the asset is sold (that is, wholesale prices, retail prices, and liquidation or "fire sale" prices are different). These prices will not necessarily be equal to current cost.

formance for five years expressed in constant dollars. This enables the reader to easily determine whether changes in these variables have kept pace with inflation. If dividends, for example, have decreased in constant dollar terms, it indicates that the purchasing power of the current dividend is less than the purchasing power distributed in past years. Similarly, if sales in nominal dollars have increased by less than the inflation rate, the summary will show decreases in constant dollar sales. Growth is very important to many investors and others who use financial information. The five-year constant dollar summary provides a new perspective on growth in an inflationary environment.

Management's Explanation and Interpretation

Statement 33 requires that management explain the constant dollar and current cost information and discuss its significance in terms of their particular situations. Users will find explanations of what the numbers mean and of the methods and techniques used in calculating the numbers. The following are some of the subjects commonly found in managements' analyses:

Problems Caused by Inflation—The problem of achieving real growth in an inflationary environment is often cited by management. They explain that increasing prices must be matched by increases in investment if a company is to maintain its operating capability or maintain its investment in terms of purchasing power. Financial information that is not adjusted for the effects of changing prices can give misleading impressions of growth. Moreover, they explain that internally financed investment can come only after payment of taxes and must compete with taxes and dividends for limited supplies of funds.

Strategies for Coping with Inflation—Management

discusses trends and summary indicators in reviewing the effectiveness of strategies of coping with inflation Two strategies for coping with inflation often discussed by management include technological developments and pricing policies. Technological developments may offset inflationary pressures by reducing the effective costs per unit of output or by improving the quality of the product or both. Pricing policies may be designed to pass rising costs to customers; the effectiveness of this strategy depends on the sensitivity of the product's demand to price increases.

Constant Dollar and Current Cost Methods— Management explains the constant dollar and current cost methods and techniques used in calculating cost of goods sold and depreciation expense.

Purchasing Power Gains or Losses on Net Monetary Items—Management often explains the calculation of the purchasing power gain or loss on net monetary items. Various interpretations of the amount will be found, including the views that the purchasing power gain can be regarded as an offset to interest expense, that incurring additional debt to produce a gain would not necessarily be beneficial, and that a gain does not represent a receipt of cash that can be used for reinvestment or distributions.

By its very nature, the management's explanation and interpretation defies attempts to present a typical example. No two such explanations are alike. Thus, the following actual examples are typical only in a broad sense. They are excerpted from an FASB Special Report, *Examples of the Use of FASB Statement No. 33, Financial Reporting and Changing Prices*, that includes many more actual examples of Statement 33 disclosures.

Storage Technology Corporation

General background

Financial statements of business enterprises presented in accordance with generally accepted accounting principles have traditionally reported amounts reflecting historical costs and dollars of varying purchasing power and accordingly do not adequately measure the effects of inflation on a business. Changing prices, particularly during periods of high inflation, can have significant effects. In recognition of the need to provide readers of financial statements with information to assist them in assessing these effects, the Financial Accounting Standards Board (FASB) issued Statement No. 33, Financial Reporting and Changing Prices, which requires that certain information about the effects of inflation on business enterprises be disclosed.

The information which follows is consistent with the requirements of Statement No. 33, and is intended to provide certain measurements of the effects of inflation on STC's operations and financial position.

Methods of measuring effects of changing prices

The two methods prescribed by the FASB for measuring the effects of changing prices were used in calculating the information which follows.

The first method provides data adjusted for "general inflation" using the Consumer Price Index for all Urban Consumers as a broad-based measure of general inflation. The objective of this approach is to provide financial information in dollars of equivalent purchasing power (constant dollars) so that revenues for each year are matched with expenses expressed in corresponding units. In addition, financial data presented for a series of years is made more comparable by reporting the amounts for each year in terms of a common measure of purchasing power.

The second method adjusts for "changes in specific prices." The objective of this method is to reflect the effects of changes in the specific prices (current costs) of the resources actually used in STC's operations, so that measures of these resources and their consumption reflect the current cost of replacing these resources, rather than the historical cost amounts actually expended to acquire them. Adjustments for changes in specific prices of property, plant and equipment were based on external price indexes closely related to the assets being measured. The current costs of inventories, computer peripheral rental equipment, spare parts for field service and related cost of sales and depreciation were based on recent manufacturing costs.

It should be noted that both of the above described methods inherently involve the use of assumptions, approximations and estimates. The results should be viewed in that context and should not be viewed as precise indicators of the effects of inflation.

Review of information presented

Supplementary financial data adjusted for the effects of changing prices

In calculating net income adjusted for general inflation and changes in specific prices, the amounts reported in the primary financial statements have been adjusted for depreciation expense (of property, plant and equipment and computer peripheral rental equipment) and those manufacturing costs related to cost of sales, service and installation. Revenues and all other operating expenses are considered to reflect the average price levels for the year and accordingly have not been adjusted. The adjustment to operating expenses related to depreciation of property, plant and equipment is not significant and has been included with the adjustment to cost of sales, service and installation.

Although the adjustments described above affect pretax income for constant dollar and current cost reporting, no adjustment has been made to the historical cost provision for income taxes because of the relationship of the various income tax codes to historical cost accounting.

The adjustments to expenses included in the primary financial statements are summarized as follows (in millions):

	Constant dollar accounting	Current cost accounting
Increase (decrease) in:		
Depreciation of property, plant and equipment	$ .7	$ .7
Depreciation of rental equipment	3.2	.1
Cost of sales, service and installation, exclusive of depreciation	14.5	(13.3)
Total increase (decrease) in expenses	$18.4	$(12.5)

The adjustment for depreciation of property, plant and equipment increased expense for both constant dollar and current cost accounting. These adjustments are less than 10% of historical cost depreciation largely because most of STC's property, plant and equipment was acquired in the last three years and therefore historical cost closely reflects current dollars.

The adjustments to depreciation of rental equipment and to cost of sales, service and installation (both of which reflect STC's manufacturing costs) reflect a $17.7 million increase in expense under constant dollar accounting and a $13.2 million reduction in expense under current cost accounting. These varying results demonstrate the differences between the constant dollar and current cost methods. Constant dollar accounting restates historical costs using the general inflation rate. Inherent in this method is the assumption that all costs increase at the same rate as the Consumer Price Index. The constant dollar method does not reflect STC's and the industry's experience wherein technological advances have offset much of the inflationary cost pressures felt in other industries. The current cost method reflects STC's ability to reduce manufacturing costs through technological advances which enable production efficiencies and component cost reductions. However, this result is not necessarily indicative of a lower future cost trend, since the factors contributing to a lowering of costs in the past may not be present in the future. Given STC's experience, it is your management's belief that the current cost method is a more appropriate method of accounting for inflation.

Included in the disclosures are two additional measures of the effects of inflation. The first measure, "gain from decline in purchasing power of net monetary liabilities," demonstrates the effect of having net monetary liabilities during a period of declining purchasing power. In 1979 this effect for both methods was a gain of $12.5 million. Net monetary liabilities include all of STC's consolidated assets and liabilities, other than inventories, computer peripheral rental equipment, spare parts for field service, property, plant and equipment, other assets, the residual portion of net investment in sales-type leases and contractual rents for future periods.

The second additional measure, "increase in current cost, net of inflation," reflects the

benefit of acquiring or holding certain nonmonetary assets (inventories, computer peripheral rental equipment, spare parts for field service and property, plant and equipment) at values less than the current year-end replacement value. The $.1 million includes a $2.8 million increase in current costs of such assets net of a $2.7 million increase related to the general rate of inflation.

Net assets, after giving effect to the above two adjustments, would be $149.6 million for constant dollar accounting and $180.6 million for current cost accounting.

Five-year comparison of selected supplementary financial data adjusted for effects of changing prices

The five-year comparison shows the effect of adjusting historical revenues to amounts expressed in terms of average 1979 dollars, as measured by the Consumer Price Index. Revenues for 1975 through 1978 would be higher than reported in the primary financial statements and the adjusted percentage increase in revenues in each of those years to 1979 would be correspondingly less. The market price per share amounts show a similar trend of slower growth in each of the earlier years to 1979 when restated to average 1979 dollars.

Supplementary financial data adjusted for the effects of changing prices for the year ended December 28, 1979 (in millions, except per share amounts)

	Primary statements	Adjusted for general inflation (constant dollar)	Adjusted for changes in specific prices (current costs)
Total revenues	$479.5	$479.5	$479.5
Cost of sales, service and installation	286.9	302.1	274.3
Depreciation of rental equipment	19.0	22.2	19.1
Other operating expenses	104.5	104.5	104.5
Total costs and expenses	410.4	428.8	397.9
Income before taxes	69.1	50.7	81.6
Provision for income taxes	29.4	29.4	29.4
Net income	$ 39.7	$ 21.3*	$ 52.2
Earnings per primary and fully diluted share	$ 1.58	$ .85*	$ 2.07
Gain from decline in purchasing power of net monetary liabilities		$ 12.5	$ 12.5
Increase in current cost, net of inflation			$ .1

*As described previously, it is management's belief that the results of the constant dollar method of measuring the effects of inflation are not appropriate based upon STC's past experience of reduced costs through technological advances.

The current cost of inventories, computer peripheral rental equipment, spare parts for field service and property, plant and equipment, net of accumulated depreciation, at December 28, 1979 and corresponding historical cost amounts are as follows (in millions):

	Inventories	Computer peripheral rental equipment	Spare parts for field service	Property, plant and equipment	Total
Current cost	$110.9	$62.4	$22.3	$78.1	$273.7
Historical cost	$110.9	$65.6	$23.9	$70.9	$271.3

Five-year comparison of selected supplementary financial data adjusted for effects of changing prices (in average 1979 dollars):

	Unadjusted for effects of changing prices	Adjustment	Adjusted total
Total revenues (in millions)			
1979	$479.5	$ —	$479.5
1978	$300.4	$33.8	$334.2
1977	$162.3	$32.1	$194.4
1976	$121.8	$33.5	$155.3
1975	$ 98.8	$34.4	$133.2

Market price per common share at end of fiscal years (after adjustments for stock dividends and stock splits):

1979	$17.13	$ (.94)	$16.19
1978	$15.38	$1.09	$16.47
1977	$ 5.44	$ .91	$ 6.35
1976	$ 2.73	$ .68	$ 3.41
1975	$ 2.26	$ .70	$ 2.96

The average consumer price indexes used in calculating the above adjustments for the effect of changing prices were as follows: 1979-217.4; 1978-195.4; 1977-181.5; 1976-170.5; 1975-161.2. Adjusted data on dividends per common share is not presented because no cash dividends have ever been paid by STC.

General Electric Company

Financial issues:
the impact of inflation

Inflation is commonly defined as a loss in value of money due to an increase in the volume of money and credit relative to available goods and services, resulting in a rise in the level of prices. Inflation in the U.S. is generally recognized to be caused by a combination of factors, including government deficits, sharp increases in energy costs, and low productivity gains including the effect of proliferating government regulations.

Although loss of purchasing power of the dollar impacts all areas of the economy, it is particularly onerous in its effect on savings — of both individuals in forms such as savings accounts, securities and pensions, and of corporations in the form of retained earnings.

For the individual, with inflation of 6% a year, the dollar saved by a person at age 50 will have lost three-fifths of its value by the time the person is age 65. With a 10% inflation rate, almost four-fifths of the dollar's value is lost in 15 years. This problem affects almost everyone, including those presently working and especially those who are on fixed incomes.

The situation is rendered even more difficult by the progressive income tax system. A Congressional staff study reports that a family of four with an income of $8,132 in 1964 would need a 1979 income of $18,918 to have kept pace with the increase in the Consumer Price Index over the years. However, the 1979 income of $18,918 puts the family into a higher tax bracket which, when coupled with increased Social Security taxes, reduces real after-tax income $1,068 below the equivalent 1964 level.

Your Company and all U.S. businesses face a similar problem. Business savings are in the form of retained earnings — the earnings a company keeps after paying employees, suppliers and vendors, and after payment of taxes to government and dividends to share owners. If a company is to continue in business, much less grow, it must be able to save or retain sufficient earnings, after providing a return to its share owners, to fund the cost of replacing — at today's inflated prices — the productive assets used up. Retention of capital in these inflationary times under existing tax laws is a challenge facing all businesses.

U.S. tax regulations permit recognition of the impact of inflation on a company's inventory costs by use of the LIFO (last-in, first-out) inventory method. In general, under the LIFO method, a company charges off to operations the current cost of inventories consumed during the year. With inflation averaging over 11% last year, the negative impact on operations of using current costs with respect to a supply of goods is substantial. Financial results are portrayed more accurately when the LIFO method is used in periods of high inflation, and GE has used LIFO for most of its U.S. manufacturing inventories for a quarter-century. The Statement of Earnings on page 32 is on that basis. As

supplementary information to that Statement of Earnings: use of the LIFO method increased 1979 and 1978 operating costs by $430.8 million and $224.1 million (to $20,330.7 million and $17,695.9 million), respectively, with a corresponding reduction of reported pre-tax profits.

Unfortunately, U.S. tax regulations fail to provide an equivalent to LIFO for the impact of inflation on a company's costs of property, plant and equipment. Instead, deductions for wear and tear on these assets are based on original purchase costs rather than today's replacement costs. In general, the resulting shortfall must be funded from after-tax earnings.

The supplementary information shown in Table 1 restates operating results to eliminate the major effects of inflation discussed above. Table 1 compares GE operating results as reported on page 32 with results adjusted in two ways. First, results are restated to show the effects of general inflation — the loss of the dollar's purchasing power — on inventories and fixed assets. The second restatement shows results restated for changes in specific prices — the current costs of replacing those assets. Your management feels that the last column in Table 1 is the more meaningful and has therefore shown, in Table 2 on page 30, five years of results on that basis, also adjusted to equivalent 1979 dollars to make the years comparable. While the techniques used are not precise, they do produce reasonable approximations.

In these earnings statements, specific adjustments are made to (1) *cost of goods sold* for the current cost of replacing inventories and (2) *depreciation* for the current costs of plant and equipment. The restatements for inventories are relatively small because GE's extensive use of LIFO accounting already largely reflects current costs in the traditional statements. However, a substantial restatement is made for the impact of inflation on fixed assets, which have relatively long lives. The $624 million of depreciation as traditionally reported, when restated for general inflation, increases to a total of $880 million. But the restatement necessary to reflect replacement of these assets at current costs grows to $980 million. The net effect of these restatements lowers reported income of $6.20 a share to $4.68 on a general inflation-adjusted basis and $4.34 on a specific current cost basis.

It is significant to note that for the five years 1975-1979, even after adjustment for inflation, your Company has shown real growth in earnings and a steady increase in share owners' equity over the entire period. After adjusting earnings for current costs and restating all years to equivalent 1979 dollars, your Company's average annual growth rate in real earnings was 21% since 1975 and 8% since 1976. This means that the growth in GE's earnings has been real, not just the product of inflation.

An important insight from these data is depicted in the pie charts at right. These show that, over the five years 1975-1979, because of inflation 10% more of GE's earnings were taxed away than appeared to have been the case using traditional financial statements. While the traditional earnings statements indicated an effective tax rate of 41% over this period, the "real" tax rate averaged 51% of profits before taxes. Consequently, earnings

General Electric Company

Table 1: supplementary information – effect of changing prices (a)

(In millions, except per-share amounts)   The notes on page 30 are an integral part of this statement.

For the year ended December 31, 1979	As reported in the traditional statements	Adjusted for general inflation	Adjusted for changes in specific prices (current costs) (b)
Sales of products and services to customers	$22,461	$22,461	$22,461
Cost of goods sold	15,991	16,093	16,074
Selling, general and administrative expense	3,716	3,716	3,716
Depreciation, depletion and amortization	624	880	980
Interest and other financial charges	258	258	258
Other income	(519)	(519)	(519)
Earnings before income taxes and minority interest	2,391	2,033	1,952
Provision for income taxes	953	953	953
Minority interest in earnings of consolidated affiliates	29	16	13
Net earnings applicable to common stock	$ 1,409	$ 1,064	$ 986
Earnings per common share	$ 6.20	$ 4.68	$ 4.34
Share owners' equity at year end (net assets) (c)	$ 7,362	$10,436	$11,153

Use of each dollar of earnings
Based on total earnings before taxes 1975-1979

As reported

Retained for growth 32¢
Taxes 41¢
Minority interest 1¢
Dividends 26¢

Adjusted for changes in specific prices (current costs)

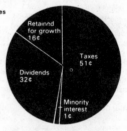

Retained for growth 16¢
Taxes 51¢
Dividends 32¢
Minority interest 1¢

retained for growth were cut in half to 16% of income before tax, not 32% as reflected in the traditional financial statements. Over the period, share owners received a measure of protection against inflation's impact as about two-thirds of after-tax earnings were distributed — equivalent to an average annual growth rate of about 8% in *real* dividends.

An area receiving special attention by management is experimentation with the use of inflation-adjusted measurements at the individual business and project level for capital budgeting. Since 1973, your Company has been experimenting with various techniques to measure the impact of inflation, to incorporate the perspectives provided by such measurements into decision-making, and to stimulate awareness by all levels of management of the need to develop constructive business strategies to deal with inflation. The objective is to ensure that investments needed for new business growth, productivity improvements and capacity expansions earn appropriate

real rates of return commensurate with the risks involved. Such supplemental measurements can assist in the entire resource allocation process, starting with initial project approval, implementation and subsequent review.

improving productivity to offset inflationary forces is a primary goal established by top management that is being stressed throughout General Electric. As discussed on the back cover of this Annual Report, the Company has committed significant levels of resources to research and development activities to accelerate innovation and increase productivity. In addition, General Electric's production base continues to be expanded and modernized through increasing investments in plant and equipment. For example, $1,262 million and $1,055 million were spent on strengthening General Electric's production base in 1979 and 1978, respectively. Imaginative and diligent coupling of production techniques and equipment is critical to the maintenance and improvement of your Company's profitability.

The General Electric Investor

General Electric Company

Table 2: supplementary information – effect of changing prices (a)

(In millions, except per-share amounts)

Current cost information in dollars of 1979 purchasing power (b)

(All amounts expressed in average 1979 dollars)	1979	1978	· 1977	1976	1975
Sales of products and services to customers	$22,461	$21,867	$20,984	$20,015	$19,022
Cost of goods sold	16,074	15,548	14,793	14,145	13,914
Selling, general and administrative expense	3,716	3,566	3,606	3,360	3,018
Depreciation, depletion and amortization	980	1,000	986	979	1,006
Interest and other financial charges	258	249	238	222	251
Other income	(519)	(466)	(467)	(350)	(235)
Earnings before income taxes and minority interest	1,952	1,970	1,828	1,659	1,068
Provision for income taxes	953	995	926	853	620
Minority interest in earnings of consolidated affiliates	13	13	20	26	26
Net earnings applicable to common stock	$ 986	$ 962	$ 882	$ 780	$ 422
Earnings per common share	$ 4.34	$ 4.22	$ 3.88	$ 3.45	$ 1.88
Share owners' equity at year end (net assets) (c)	$11,153	$11,020	$10,656	$10,526	$10,056
Other inflation information					
Average Consumer Price Index (1967 = 100)	217.4	195.4	181.5	170.5	161.2
(Loss)/gain in general purchasing power of net monetary items	$(209)	$(128)	$ (61)	$ (20)	$ 19
Dividends declared per common share	2.75	2.78	2.52	2.17	2.16
Market price per common share at year end	47⅞	50½	58¼	69⅜	60¼

Notes to supplementary information — Tables 1 and 2

(a) This information has been prepared in accordance with requirements of the Financial Accounting Standards Board (FASB). Proper use of this information requires an understanding of certain basic concepts and definitions.

The heading "As reported in the traditional statements" refers to information drawn directly from the financial statements presented on pages 32 to 44. This information is prepared using the set of generally accepted accounting principles which renders an accounting based on the number of actual dollars involved in transactions, with no recognition given to the fact that the value of the dollar changes over time.

The heading "Adjusted for general inflation" refers to information prepared using a different approach to transactions involving inventory and property, plant and equipment assets. Under this procedure, the number of dollars involved in transactions at different dates are all restated to equivalent amounts in terms of the general purchasing power of the dollar as it is measured by the Consumer Price Index for all Urban Consumers (CPI-U). For example, $1,000 invested in a building asset in 1967 would be restated to its 1979 dollar purchasing power equivalent of $2,174 to value the asset and calculate depreciation charges. Similarly, 1978 purchases of non-LIFO inventory sold in 1979 would be accounted for at their equivalent in terms of 1979 dollars, rather than in terms of the actual number of dollars spent.

The heading "Adjusted for changes in specific prices (current costs)" refers to information prepared using yet another approach to transactions involving inventory and property, plant and equipment assets. In this case, rather than restating to dollars of the same general purchasing power, estimates of current costs of the assets are used.

In presenting results of either or the supplementary accounting methods for more than one year, "real" trends are more evident when results for all years are expressed in terms of the general purchasing power of the dollar for a designated period. Results of such restatements are generally called "constant dollar" presentations. In the five-year presentations shown above, dollar results for earlier periods have been restated to their equivalent number of constant dollars of 1979 general purchasing power (CPI-U basis).

Since none of these restatements is allowable for tax purposes under existing regulations, income tax amounts are the same as in the traditional statements (but expressed in constant dollars in the five-year summary).

There are a number of other terms and concepts which may be of interest in assessing the significance of the supplementary information shown in Tables 1 and 2. However, it is management's opinion that the basic concepts discussed above are the most significant for the reader to have in mind while reviewing this information.

(b) Principal types of information used to adjust for changes in specific prices (current costs) are (1) for inventory costs, GE-generated indices of price changes for specific goods and services, and (2) for property, plant and equipment, externally generated indices of price changes for major classes of assets.

(c) At December 31, 1979, the current cost of inventory was $5,251 million, and of property, plant and equipment was $7,004 million. Estimated current costs applicable to the sum of such amounts held during all or part of 1979 increased by approximately $1,111 million, which was $329 million less than the $1,440-million increase which could be expected because of general inflation.

Annual Report 1979

Analysis

Analysis of financial information is beyond the scope of this book. There are many ratios, comparisons, and other techniques that are used to evaluate financial information. Many existing techniques will be enhanced by use of the new information that reflects the effects of changing prices. Additional new techniques will undoubtedly be developed as analysts gain familiarity with the new data. A few examples of commonly used ratios that may be enhanced by substituting the new information are described below.

Return on Equity

A commonly used ratio is income divided by net assets (that is, shareholder's equity). This measure, also useful in comparing companies, is intended to indicate how effectively a company is able to use its net assets to generate income. In computing a revised return on equity, an analyst could use any of the performance measures discussed above. The return figure might be, for example, current cost operating income, and the equity figure would be net assets computed on the same basis (current cost net assets). If income is measured in a way that allows for changes in purchasing power, the rate of return will be lower than under traditional measures; users will need to develop new standards for evaluating rates of return adjusted for changing prices.

Price/Earnings Ratio

Many investors who compare alternative stock investments compute the ratio of the price of the stock to the earnings per share. This ratio indicates how much the potential investor must pay to acquire earnings of one dollar. Price/earnings ratios may be computed and compared using any of the new performance measures described earlier.

Dividend Payout Ratio

The dividend payout ratio is the ratio of dividends paid to income. It indicates how much of the income stream is currently distributed to owners and how much is being retained in the business. A low dividend payout ratio may indicate that a company has the capacity to increase dividends in the future or that the dividend is unlikely to be reduced if earnings temporarily decline. Because of the "distributable income" idea, investors may be particularly interested in computing this ratio using current cost operating income or current cost operating income plus holding gains and losses.

Net Asset Value per Share

Some investors are interested in investing in companies because of the value of the assets they hold. They look for undervalued stocks—those where the price of the stock does not fully reflect the perceived value of the underlying assets of the company. They can compute adjusted net asset value per share on a current cost basis and compare the result to stock prices. Current costs are not a direct measure of share "value," but investors may regard them as useful in making their own estimates of value based on knowledge of the kind of assets the company holds.

Leverage

Investors may be interested in calculating a leverage ratio—the ratio of existing debt to equity—to evaluate the capacity of the company to increase its borrowing. Leverage is also considered useful in assessing risk involved in an investment. Current cost measures of assets may be useful for such purposes. For example, a company that owns real estate purchased 20 years ago for $50,000 is likely to have a different borrowing capacity from that of a company that owns real estate purchased 2 years ago for $50,000. That difference would show up from different perspectives in both constant dollar and current cost measures of assets but not in historical cost measures. In this sense, both constant dollar and current cost information may enhance the ability of readers to compare different companies.

PART II

More about Income, with Illustrations

INCOME

Part I of this book observes that people have an intuitive understanding of what is meant by *income* even though they may not be able to state or agree on a precise definition. In fact, although people generally agree about many of the characteristics of *income*, there is controversy about how it should be measured and how the word *income*, and certain other terms such as *earnings*, should be used. Some construe the term broadly to include the entire increase in net assets excluding only the effect of payments to or from stockholders (for example, dividends). The Board has defined the term *comprehensive income* to refer specifically to that concept.

Others believe that the term *income* should be construed more narrowly to exclude some types of changes in net assets. They may prefer the more specific term *operating income* or the term *earnings*. In particular, relating this concept to Statement 33, they may not consider *holding gains and losses* or *monetary gains and losses* to be part of income.

The FASB has undertaken the task of defining *income*, or related terms such as *earnings*, as part of its conceptual framework project. Pending completion of that task, the term *income*, by itself, is ambiguous. Nevertheless, it may be useful to discuss some of the ideas encompassed by *operating income* and the other components of *comprehensive income* in order to understand Statement 33.

First of all, income is desirable; income is preferred to lack of income or to negative income (losses); and more income is preferred to less. Income represents success, since one of the objectives (some say the *only* objective) of a business enterprise is to make income (or *profits*). Conversely, lack of income indicates lack of success.

Closely related to the idea of income as an element of success is the concept of *performance*. If the objective of business is to make income, then the *performance* of the business may be evaluated by measuring or determining the income earned. Income is generally assumed to be quantifiable, as implied by the use of the phrase *measurement of income*. That is, we may obtain more information about income than its presence or absence. We may ask, "How much?" not just "Is it present?"

Measurement of income also requires that we have a unit of measure. The units used are dollars or other units of money, such as yen or francs. The discussion of constant dollar accounting in Part I points out some of the difficulties that may arise when the size of the measuring unit changes over time. That discussion suggests that the characteristic of income that we really want to measure is *purchasing power*. In other words, income in dollars is not an objective in itself; income (or money) is desired because it represents the power to purchase things that people want. Income is, therefore, related to the ability to satisfy wants, or to consume.

Income is also related to increases in the assets (net of liabilities) owned by an individual or an enterprise. If a business has more net assets at the end of a period than it had at the beginning (after adjusting for any new investment from and distributions to owners), it has income (at least in the sense of *comprehensive income*). This makes it clear that measurement of income is related to measurement of assets and liabilities. A detailed discussion of the measurement of assets and liabilities is a subject that is beyond the scope of this book. However, we discuss several different measurements in Part I, including historical cost and current cost. Each measurement attribute applied to assets generates a corresponding measurement of income. It is possible that more than one income measure might be needed.

The idea that there may be more than one income number simultaneously is a little unfamiliar but not too complicated. Income might be compared to a child's growth—defined as an increase in "bigness." We might measure growth as increases in the attribute *height* or as increases in the attribute *weight*. We might also be interested in more specific, narrower measures, such as shoe size. To fully understand the growth of a child, we might decide to measure and record both height and weight, and perhaps other attributes. Multiple measures of income may be similarly useful.

Income (especially *comprehensive income*) is also described as an increase in "well-offness." Measurement of "well-offness," however, presents the same problems as measurement of net assets.

In an accounting sense, operating income may be defined as the excess of revenues over expenses. Since revenues are increases in net assets and expenses are decreases in net assets, there is a close relationship between this and the increase in net assets discussed above.

Income may also be described as return *on* investment, as opposed to return *of* investment. In this view, business is a process of investing money in hopes of obtaining an eventual return of the investment plus an additional amount. Thus, income is the amount left over after the original investment is recouped.

Income of a business is related to, but usually not the same as, cash flow. Revenues generally represent cash inflows, although under accrual accounting we may record the revenue in a time period earlier or later than the period of the related inflow. Expenses are similarly related to cash outflows. Information about cash flows may be useful, along with other information, in assessing performance. Some cash flows, however, such as cash paid to buy a building or cash received in payment of a receivable, are not components of income.

But how do these ideas about *income* (however defined) relate to the financial information required by Statement 33? Part I of this book (page 25) identifies four components of information about performance— constant dollar operating income, current cost operating income, holding gain or loss, and monetary gain or loss. Part I also identifies (page 35) several combinations of those components that may be useful in understanding performance. The different perspectives on a company's performance that can be obtained from the four components and combinations thereof are reflections of the various ways of looking at what the Board has defined as *comprehensive income* and its components.

ILLUSTRATIONS

The rest of Part II consists of two simplified examples that illustrate the meaning and computation of Statement 33 information.

Millander, Inc.

Millander, Inc. buys grain and mills it into flour. The company's transactions and certain other information are summarized below.

MILLANDER, INC.

Date	Transaction	Amount	Cash Balance	CPI
1/01/X1	Sell stock	$1,500	$1,500	100
1/01/X1	Purchase mill	$1,000	$ 500	
1/01/X1	Purchase 1000 lbs. of grain	$ 500	$ 0	
6/30/X1	Sell 1000 lbs. of flour	$1,100	$1,100	110
7/01/X1	Purchase 1000 lbs. of grain	$ 750	$ 350	
12/31/X1	Pay dividend	$ 100	$ 250	120
6/30/X2	Sell 1000 lbs. of flour	$1,350	$1,600	135
12/31/X2	Pay dividend	$ 100	$1,500	150

The mill has a useful life of two years with no salvage value. The cost of a new mill was:

1/01/X1	$1,000
6/30/X1 (average for year)	$1,250
12/31/X1	$1,500
6/30/X2 (average for year)	$1,750
12/31/X2	$2,000

The price of grain (per 1000 lbs.) was:

1/01/X1	$ 500
6/30/X1	$ 750
12/31/X1	$ 900
6/30/X2	$1,000
12/31/X2	$1,200

At 12/31/X2 Millander had cash of $1,500 and its mill was worn out.

Millander's summarized historical cost income statement and relevant portions of its Statement 33 disclosures are shown on pages 58 and 59.

MILLANDER, INC.
Income Statement
(Historical Cost in Nominal Dollars)

	Year Ended December 31,	
	X1	**X2**
Sales	$1,100	$1,350
Cost of grain sold	500	750
Depreciation	500	500
Net income	$ 100	$ 100

MILLANDER, INC.
Supplemental Information
Year Ended December 31, X1

	In Average X1 Dollars		In Average X2 Dollars*	
	Current Cost	Constant Dollar	Current Cost	Constant Dollar
Sales	$1,100	$1,100	$1,350	$1,350
Cost of grain sold	750	550	920	675
Depreciation	625	550	767	675
(Loss) from operations	$ (275)	$ 0	$ (337)	$ 0
Increase in current costs of inventory and mill (nominal holding gains)	$ 775		$ 951	
Portion of increase due to general inflation	288		353	
Excess of increase in current cost over general inflation (net holding gains)	$ 487		$ 597	
Gain (loss) in purchasing power on net monetary items	$ (29)	$ (29)	$ (36)	$ (36)

---

*The columns showing information for the year X1 translated into average X2 dollars are included to show how amounts reconcile for the two-year period. They would not ordinarily be presented in the company's report.

MILLANDER, INC.
Supplemental Information
Year Ended December 31, X2
(In Average X2 Dollars)

	Current Cost	Constant Dollar
Sales	$1,350	$1,350
Cost of grain sold	1,000	920
Depreciation	875	675
(Loss) from operations	$ (525)	$ (245)
Increase in current costs of inventory and mill	$ 225	
Portion of increase due to general inflation	205	
Excess of increase in current cost over general inflation (net holding gains or losses)	20	
Gain (loss) in purchasing power on net monetary items	$ (191)	$ (191)

Millander, Inc. had net income, based on the traditional historical cost nominal dollar approach, of $100 in each year. That reflects the fact that the company earned an increased number of nominal dollars. Since it distributed $200 in dividends and ended the 2-year period with cash of $1,500 equal to the initial $1,500 investment, the company did earn 200 nominal dollars.

Over the two years, the company suffered a constant dollar operating loss. Since the company held cash balances during an inflationary period, it also had a monetary loss. In terms of purchasing power, an investor could evaluate the investment in Millander, Inc. as follows (in average X2 dollars):

	Nominal Dollars	Conversion Factor	Average X2 Dollars
Initial investment (1,500 1/1/X1 dollars)	$(1,500)	135/100	$(2,025)
Year-1 dividend (100 12/31/X1 dollars)	$ 100	135/120	113
Year-2 dividend (100 12/31/X2 dollars)	$ 100	135/150	90
Ending cash (1,500 12/31/X2 dollars)	$ 1,500	135/150	1,350
Net loss in purchasing power			$ (472)

The investors' purchasing power loss is also shown by the constant dollar schedules. Using the same units—average X2 dollars—the company's constant dollar results may be summarized as follows:

X1	Operating loss	$ 0
X1	Monetary loss	(36)
X2	Operating loss	(245)
X2	Monetary loss	(191)
	Total	$(472)

The current cost operating losses indicate that the company's revenues were not sufficient to cover the replacement of the grain sold and the mill used in production. At 12/31/X2, Millander had cash of $1,500. To remain in the business with the capacity to produce the same amount of flour, it must have $2,000 for a new machine and $1,200 for a supply of grain.

Millander, Inc. also reported net holding gains of $597 and $20 (both in average X2 dollars) in X1 and X2. That reflects the fact that the prices of the assets the company held—the mill and grain—increased faster than the general price level, especially in year X1. The rates of increase may be summarized as follows:

	Mill	Grain	CPI
X1	50%	80%	20%
X2	33%	33%	25%

A reconciliation of current cost results, similar to that presented above for constant dollars, may be performed as follows (in average X2 dollars):

X1	Operating loss	$(337)
X1	Net holding gain	597
X1	Monetary loss	(36)
X2	Operating loss	(525)
X2	Net holding gain	20
X2	Monetary loss	(191)
	Total	$(472)

Carcas Beef Company

The example of Carcas Beef Company is somewhat more complex than the preceding Millander example. It includes details of how the disclosures are calculated from the facts given because one way to understand the new information is to see how it is computed.

The company has 1 fixed asset, a warehouse with an estimated useful life of 20 years purchased on December 31, 1968 for $2,000. At December 31, 1978, the company's traditional historical cost balance sheet appeared as follows:

Assets:	
Cash	$ 100
Inventory (100 units purchased on June 30, 1978 for $9 each)	900
Warehouse—	
Cost	2,000
Accumulated depreciation	(1,000)
Total	$2,000
Liabilities and Equity:	
Note payable at 12%, due in 1985	$1,000
Equity	1,000
Total	$2,000

The company uses the "first-in-first-out" method of accounting for inventory and the straight-line depreciation method.

The following information about cash transactions and price changes during 1979 and 1980 provides the basis for the supplementary disclosures (as required by Statement 33) that appear in Tables 1, 2, and 3.

	1978	1979	1980
Sales, units (occurring evenly through the year)		200	200
Average sales price		$ 15	$ 18
Sales, nominal dollars		$3,000	$3,600
Purchases (on June 30) — units		200	200
— price		$ 10	$ 15
Cash expenses (including interest of $120)		$ 470	$ 520
Dividends paid per share		$ 2.00	$ 2.10
Shares outstanding		100	100
Consumer price index — December 31	203	230	264
— June 30*	195	217	249
Estimated current cost at December 31			
Inventory units	$ 9.50	$ 11	$ 18
Warehouse	$5,000	$6,000	$7,000
CPI at December 31, 1968 = 104			

*Equal to average for year.

The following tables present the basic information required by Statement 33. Management's explanation of the meaning of the information is not included as part of this example. (See pages 40-46 for an example of management's explanation.) The tables presented are:

Table 1—Supplemental information about income adjusted for changing prices for 1979 (as it would appear in the 1979 annual report)

Table 2—Supplemental information about income adjusted for changing prices (as it would appear in the 1980 annual report)

Table 3—Two-year comparison of selected supplementary information adjusted for the effects of changing prices (as it might appear in the 1980 annual report, except that five years of data would be shown for some line items)

In reviewing the information, notice that the information in Table 1 for 1979 is not the same as the 1979 information in Table 3. This is because in Table 3 the 1979 information has been expressed in average 1980 dollars to make it comparable to the 1980 information. The information in Table 1 is as it would appear in the 1979 annual report and is expressed in average 1979 dollars. Except for the units used (the size of the dollars), the information *is* the same in both tables.

Table 1

CARCAS BEEF COMPANY
INCOME ADJUSTED FOR CHANGING PRICES
For the Year Ended December 31, 1979

	Historical Cost	Constant Dollar*	Current Cost*
Sales	$3,000	$3,000	$3,000
Cost of sales	1,900	2,002	2,050
Depreciation	100	209	275
Interest	120	120	120
Other expenses	350	350	350
Income from operations	$ 530	$ 319	$ 205
Purchasing power gain on net amount owed		$ 94	$ 94
Increase in specific prices (current cost) of inventories and warehouse during the year (nominal holding gain)			$ 675
Effect of increase in general price level			453
Excess of increase in specific prices over increase in general price level (net holding gain)			$ 222

---

*Stated in average 1979 dollars.

Note: At December 31, 1979, current cost of inventory was $1,100 and current cost of the warehouse (net of accumulated depreciation of $3,300) was $2,700. These amounts are expressed in *year-end* 1979 dollars.

Table 2

CARCAS BEEF COMPANY
INCOME ADJUSTED FOR CHANGING PRICES
For the Year Ended December 31, 1980

	Historical Cost	Constant Dollar*	Current Cost*
Sales	$3,600	$3,600	$3,600
Cost of sales	2,500	2,647	2,900
Depreciation	100	239	325
Interest	120	120	120
Other expenses	400	400	400
Income (loss) from operations	$ 480	$ 194	$ (145)
Purchasing power gain on net amount owed		$ 87	$ 87
Increase in specific prices (current cost) of inventories and warehouse during the year (nominal holding gain)			$1,025
Effect of increase in general price level			575
Excess of increase in specific prices over increase in general price level (net holding gain)			$ 450

*Stated in average 1980 dollars.

Note: At December 31, 1980, current cost of inventory was $1,800 and current cost of the warehouse (net of accumulated depreciation of $4,200) was $2,800. These amounts are expressed in *year-end* 1980 dollars.

Table 3

CARCAS BEEF COMPANY
COMPARISON OF SELECTED SUPPLEMENTARY FINANCIAL DATA
ADJUSTED FOR EFFECTS OF CHANGING PRICES

	Years Ended December 31,	
	1980	**1979**
Net sales and other operating revenues:		
At historical cost (as reported)	$3,600	$3,000
In average 1980 dollars	$3,600	$3,442
Historical cost information (as reported):		
Income from continuing operations	$ 480	$ 530
Income from continuing operations per common share	$ 4.80	$ 5.30
Net assets at year-end	$1,600	$1,330
Constant dollar information (historical cost information adjusted for general inflation):*		
Income from continuing operations	$ 194	$ 366
Income from continuing operations per common share	$ 1.94	$ 3.66
Net assets at year-end	$2,755	$2,685
Current cost information:*		
Income (loss) from continuing operations	$ (145)	$ 235
Income (loss) from continuing operations per common share	$ (1.45)	$ 2.35
Excess of increase in specific prices over increase in general price level	$ 450	$ 255
Net assets at year-end	$3,678	$3,497
Gain on net monetary liabilities*	$ 87	$ 108
Cash dividends declared per common share:		
In nominal dollars, as reported	$ 2.10	$ 2.00
In average 1980 dollars	$ 2.10	$ 2.29
Market price per common share at year-end:		
In nominal dollars	$36.00	$33.00
In average 1980 dollars	$33.95	$35.73
Average consumer price index	249	217

*In average 1980 dollars.

Analysis

The example of Carcas Beef Company illustrates a situation involving both fixed assets and debt. The company's current costs increased at a rate slightly higher than inflation in 1979 and much higher in 1980. The detailed computation of the disclosures from the facts given is shown in the next section. A few observations on how the information might be analyzed or used follow.

Net Assets

The analyst may be interested in the assets the company owns. Using the information on net assets from Table 3, the net assets per share can be computed as follows (for 1980):

	Current Cost	Constant Dollar
Net assets	$3,678	$2,755
Net assets per share	$36.78	$27.55

These amounts are analogous to the historical cost amount called *book value per share*, which for this company is $16.00. The analyst may want to compare these numbers with the company's stock price at December 31, 1980, as shown in Table 3. The most appropriate number for such a comparison is the stock price in the same units as the net asset number, average 1980 dollars. From Table 3, this amount is $33.95 at December 31, 1980.

Return on Equity and Price/Earnings (PE) Ratio

Combining performance and net asset information, the analyst can compute return on equity for both 1979 and 1980. The analyst can also compute adjusted PE ratios using the new information. Some examples of these computations are shown below.

Computation of Return on Equity

Based on Current Cost Operating Income

| | (In Average 1980 Dollars) | |
	1980	1979
Current cost operating income	$ (145)	$ 235
Average net assets, current cost	$3,587	$3,420
Return on equity	*	6.9%

*Not meaningful.

Based on Current Cost Operating Income + Net Holding Gain + Monetary Gain

| | (In Average 1980 Dollars) | |
	1980	1979
Current cost operating income	$ (145)	$ 235
Net holding gain	450	255
Monetary gain	87	108
Total	$ 392	$ 598
Average net assets, current cost	$3,587	$3,420
Return on equity	10.9%	17.5%

Similar computations may be made using constant dollar operating income or constant dollar operating income plus the monetary gain and average constant dollar net assets.

Computation of Price/Earnings Ratio

Price/earnings ratios may be computed using any of the performance measures and the price of the company's stock. Ideally, the ratio should be computed using the same units in both the numerator and denominator. For example, assume an analyst wanted to compute a price/earnings ratio based on constant dollar operating income plus the monetary gain. That figure for 1980 from either Table 2 or Table 3 is $281.00 or $2.81 per share, expressed in average 1980 dollars. If the analyst is making the computation in April 1981 when the price of Carcas Beef Company stock is $40.00 and the CPI has advanced to 270, the computation might be made as follows:

Constant dollar operating income + monetary gain in average 1980 dollars	$2.81
CPI April 1981/CPI average 1980	x 270/249
In April 1981 dollars	= $3.05
Stock price in April 1981 dollars	$40.00
Divided by (per above)	÷ $3.05
PE ratio	= 13.1X

Alternatively, the computation could have been made by translating the stock price into average 1980 dollars ($40.00 x 249/270 = $36.89) and dividing by $2.81

($36.89 ÷ $2.81 = 13.1). PE ratios can also be computed using other measures of performance provided by Statement 33, such as current cost operating income.

Dividend Payout Ratio

The analyst is also interested in dividends and can compute the dividend payout ratio as shown below. Because current cost operating income is sometimes considered to be an approximation of "distributable income" (the amount that the company could distribute and still retain enough of its revenues to maintain its productive capacity), the analyst might elect to use that income measure. The information is available from Table 3.

	1980	1979
Dividends	$ 2.10	$2.29
Current cost operating income (loss)	$(1.45)	$2.35
Ratio	*	.97

*Not meaningful.

Trend of Dividends and Stock Price

Using the information in Table 3, the analyst can review the increase (or decrease) of dividends and the year-end stock price in real (inflation-adjusted) terms. In nominal (unadjusted) dollars, the dividend was increased from $2.00 in 1979 to $2.10 in 1980, an increase of 5%. Because the inflation rate was higher than 5% (14.7% in the example) the purchasing power of the dividend declined. The inflation-adjusted dividend (in 1980 dollars) declined from $2.29 in 1979 to $2.10 in 1980. On the same basis, the nominal increase of $3.00 per share in the stock price becomes a "real" decrease of $1.78.

Trend of Sales

From the same table, the analyst can review the "real" increase in the company's sales. In nominal dollars, the increase in sales was 20%, from $3,000 to $3,600. Adjusting for the declining purchasing power of the dollar shows an increase of 4.6%, from $3,442 to $3,600 in 1980 dollars.

How the Numbers Are Calculated

Tables 1, 2, and 3 show Carcas Beef Company's information adjusted for changing prices. The following section describes the calculations performed in arriving at these amounts.

1979 Constant Dollar Amounts in Table 1

Cost of Sales

Units Sold	Date Purchased	Historical Cost	Conversion Factor*	Average 1979 Dollars
100	6/30/78	$ 900	217/195	$1,002
100	6/30/79	$1,000	217/217	1,000
				$2,002

*CPI 1979 Average
   CPI Date

Depreciation

The warehouse was purchased on 12/31/68 for $2,000. Restating this amount in terms of average 1979 dollars, we multiply by the ratio of the average 1979 CPI and the 12/31/68 CPI, or

$$\$2,000 \times 217/104 = \$4,173$$

$$\text{Depreciation expense} = 1/20 \times \$4,173 = \$209$$

Cash

The cash account was analyzed before calculating the 1979 (Table 1) and 1980 (Table 2) gains on net amount owed.

Analysis of Cash

Balance 1/1/79		$ 100
Sales 1979	$ 3,000	
Purchases 1979	(2,000)	
Expenses, including interest	(470)	
Cash flow from operations	530	
Dividends paid	(200)	
Total		330
Balance 1/1/80		430
Sales 1980	$ 3,600	
Purchases 1980	(3,000)	
Expenses, including interest	(520)	
Cash flow from operations	80	
Dividends paid	(210)	
Total		(130)
Balance 12/31/80		$ 300

The following shows how the gain on net amount owed was calculated:

Purchasing Power Gain on Net Amount Owed for 1979

Date	Note	Historical Cost - Cash =	Net Liability	Conversion Factor*	Average 1979 Dollars
1/1/79	$1,000	$100	$ 900	217/203	$ 962
Change		$330	$(330)	assumed to be average 1979 dollars	(330)
12/31/79	$1,000	$430	$ 570	217/230	(538)
					$ 94

*CPI 1979 Average
   CPI Date

1979 Current Cost Amounts in Table 1

Cost of Sales

Current cost at 1/1/79 (per unit)	$ 9.50
Current cost at 12/31/79 (per unit)	11.00
	$20.50
	÷ 2
Average 1979 current cost	$10.25

Average 1979 current cost x units sold = cost of sales
$10.25 x 200 units = $2,050

Depreciation

Current cost of warehouse:

Current cost at 1/1/79	$ 5,000
Current cost at 12/31/79	6,000
	$11,000
	÷2
Average 1979 current cost	$ 5,500
Depreciation expense ($5,500 x 1/20)	$ 275

Holding Gains

The computation of the holding gain is shown in three parts:

1.   Holding gain associated with inventory
2.   Holding gain associated with the warehouse
3.   Nominal holding gain and net holding gain

Inventory

	Current Cost	Conversion Factor*	Average 1980 Dollars
Balance 1/1/79 (100 @ $9.50)	$ 950	217/203	$ 1,016
Purchase 6/30/79 (200 @ $10.00)	2,000		2,000
Cost of sales (200 @ $10.25)	(2,050)		(2,050)
Balance 12/31/79 (100 @ $11.00)	(1,100)	217/230	(1,038)
Increase in current cost of inventory	$ 200		$ 72

Warehouse

	Current Cost Net of Depreciation	Conversion Factor*	Average 1979 Dollars
1/1/79	$ 2,500	217/203	$ 2,672
Depreciation	(275)		(275)
12/31/79	(2,700)	217/230	(2,547)
Increase in current cost of warehouse	$ 475		$ 150

Inventory and Warehouse Combined

	Inventory	Warehouse	Total
Nominal holding gain	$200	$475	$675
Net holding gain	$ 72	$150	222
Increase due to general inflation			$453

*CPI 1980 Average

   CPI Date

1980 Constant Dollar Amounts in Table 2

Cost of Sales

Units Sold	Date Purchased	Historical Cost	Conversion Factor*	Average 1980 Dollars
100	6/30/79	$1,000	249/217	$1,147
100	6/30/80	$1,500	249/249	1,500
				$2,647

Depreciation

Restatement of warehouse cost to average
1980 dollars
$2,000 x 249/104 = $4,788

Depreciation expense
1/20 x $4,788 = $239

Purchasing Power Gain on Net Amount Owed

(See page 72 for an analysis of cash.)

		Historical Cost			
Date	Note	- Cash =	Net Liability	Conversion Factor*	Average 1980 Dollars
1/1/80	$1,000	$ 430	$570	249/230	$ 617
Change		$(130)	$130	assumed to be average 1980 dollars	130
12/31/80	$1,000	$ 300	$700	249/264	(660)
					$ 87

*CPI 1980 Average
  CPI Date

1980 Current Cost Amounts in Table 2

Cost of sales

Current cost at 1/1/80 (per unit)	$11.00
Current cost at 12/31/80 (per unit)	18.00
	29.00
	÷ 2
Average 1980 current cost	$14.50

Average 1980 current cost x unit sold = cost of sales

$14.50 x 200 units = $2,900

Depreciation

Current cost of warehouse:

Current cost at 1/1/80	$ 6,000
Current cost at 12/31/80	7,000
	$13,000
	÷ 2
Average 1980 current cost	$ 6,500
Depreciation expense (1/20 x $6,500)	$ 325

Holding gain

The computation of the holding gain is shown in three parts:

1. Holding gain associated with inventory
2. Holding gain associated with warehouse
3. Nominal holding gain and net holding gain

Inventory

	Current Cost	Conversion Factor*	Average 1980 Dollars
Balance 1/1/80 (100 @ $11.00)	$ 1,100	249/230	$ 1,191
Purchase 6/30/80 (200 @ $15.00)	3,000		3,000
Cost of sales (200 @ $14.50)	(2,900)		(2,900)
Balance 12/31/80 (100 @ $18.00)	(1,800)	249/264	(1,698)
Increase in current cost of inventory	$ 600		$ 407

Warehouse

	Current Cost Net of Depreciation	Conversion Factor*	Average 1980 Dollars
1/1/80	$ 2,700	249/230	$ 2,923
Depreciation	(325)		(325)
12/31/80	(2,800)	249/264	(2,641)
Increase in current cost of warehouse	$ 425		$ 43

Inventory and Warehouse Combined

	Inventory	Warehouse	Total
Nominal holding gain	$600	$425	$1,025
Net holding gain	$407	$ 43	450
Increase due to general inflation			$ 575

*CPI 1980 Average
    CPI Date

1980 Data in Table 3

Net Assets at Year-End

	Historical Cost	Constant Dollar	Current Cost
Cash	$ 300	$ 300	$ 300
Warehouse	2,000	5,077 (a)	7,000
Accumulated depreciation	(1,200)	(3,046) (a)	(4,200) (d)
Inventory	1,500	1,590 (b)	1,800 (e)
Note payable	(1,000)	(1,000)	(1,000)
Net assets in year-end dollars	$ 1,600	$ 2,921	$ 3,900
Conversion factor		249/264 (c)	249/264 (c)
Net assets in average 1980 dollars		$ 2,755	$ 3,678

(a) $2,000 x 264/104 = $5,077
        Accumulated depreciation = $5,077 x 12/20 = $3,046
(b) $1,500 x 264/249 = $1,590
(c)   CPI average 1980/CPI 12/31/80
(d)   12/20 x $7,000 = $4,200
(e)   100 units @ $18

1979 Data in Table 3

The ratio: 249/217 (CPI 1980 average divided by CPI 1979 average) has been used in restating the 1979 items in 1980 dollars, except for the following:

Net Assets at Year-End

	Historical Cost	Constant Dollar	Current Cost
Cash	$ 430	$ 430	$ 430
Warehouse	2,000	4,423 (a)	6,000
Accumulated depreciation	(1,100)	(2,433) (a)	(3,300) (d)
Inventory	1,000	1,060 (b)	1,100 (e)
Note payable	(1,000)	(1,000)	(1,000)
Net assets in year-end dollars	$ 1,330	$2,480	$3,230
Conversion factor		249/230 (c)	249/230 (c)
Net assets in average 1980 dollars		$2,685	$3,497

(a) $2,000 x 230/104 = $4,423
     Accumulated depreciation = $4,423 x 11/20 = $2,433
(b) $1,000 x 230/217 = $1,060
(c) CPI average 1980/CPI 12/31/79
(d) 11/20 x $6,000 = $3,300
(e) 100 units @ $11

Market Price per Common Share at Year-End and Dividends per Share

	Nominal Dollar	Conversion Factor*	Average 1980 Dollars
Price	$33.00 x	249/230 =	$35.73
Dividends	2.00 x	249/217 =	$ 2.29

*CPI 1980 Average
     CPI Date

Appendix

ADDITIONAL READINGS

This book is intended to be an introduction to the subject of accounting for changing prices. Readers who are interested in exploring the subject further may wish to start with Statement 33 itself, especially paragraphs 116-155 which address the usefulness of the required information. A few of the other available references are listed below.

Davidson, Sidney; Stickney, Clyde P.; and Weil, Roman L. *Inflation Accounting*. New York: McGraw-Hill, Inc., 1976.

Edwards, Edgar O., and Bell, Philip W. *The Theory and Measurement of Business Income*. Berkeley and Los Angeles: University of California Press, 1961.

FASB Special Report, *Examples of the Use of FASB Statement No. 33, Financial Reporting and Changing Prices*. Stamford, Conn.: FASB, November 1980.

Goldschmidt, Y., and Admon, K. *Profit Measurement During Inflation*. New York: John Wiley & Sons, Inc., 1977.

Hendriksen, Eldon S. *Accounting Theory*. 3d ed. Homewood, Ill: Richard D. Irwin, Inc., 1977.

Largay, James A., III, and Livingstone, John Leslie. *Accounting for Changing Prices*. Santa Barbara, Calif.: John Wiley & Sons, Inc., 1976.

Schultz, Helen E. *Economic Calculation Under Infla-
    tion.* Indianapolis: Liberty Press, 1976.

Sterling, Robert R. *Toward a Science of Accounting.*
    Houston: Scholars Book Co., 1979.

Wanless, P. T., and Forrester, D. A. R., eds. *Readings in
    Inflation Accounting.* Chichester, England: John
    Wiley & Sons Ltd., 1979.